Public Speaking

Simple Steps to Improve Your Skills

TIM HERRERA

© 2014 Tim Herrera, Sacramento, California

All rights reserved. No part of this book may be reproduced or transmitted in any form or by any means without written permission from the author.

Table of Contents

Introduction 10
You're not alone. Lots of people fear public speaking..........15
Why being a good public speaker is important. 21
What's your point? 27
Know your audience. 35
Know your material. 41
Know your room. 47
Tell them what you are going to tell them. 55
Keep it simple. 63
Imagine yourself giving a really, really good speech. 69
Be happy to be there. 77
Calm down. No one's going to hurt you. 83
The people listening want to like you. 89
Use personal stories. 95
Use humor. 103
Make a mistake? Move On! 111
Watch your body. 117
Watch the clock! 123
Use notes rather than scripts. 129
Engage the audience. 135
Practice. A lot. And then practice some more. 143
Speak in public as much as you can. 149
About the author. 155
Tim's other books. 157
Thank you! 159
References. 161

Words are, of course, the most powerful drug used by mankind.
~ Rudyard Kipling

Introduction

Some people get really freaked out if they have to speak in public. Don't worry if you're one of those people. It's normal. The good news is that you can do something to overcome your fear of speaking in public whether it's in front of small groups of friends in a casual setting, a medium sized group in a work environment or really large groups of total strangers out in public.

There's nothing really magical about getting better at public speaking. It's just a matter of time and effort. You can do it. You just don't realize it yet. But you will.

Are you a salesperson who wants to make pitches before large crowds but you struggle with doing that? Are you uncomfortable even speaking in front of a small group of friends? Do you want to get noticed more by your bosses at work and know that developing your public speaking skills will lead you in the right direction? Are you looking for ways to build your self-confidence?

If you have answered "yes" to any of those questions then this book will help you.

Let's face it. There will be times in your life, both personal and professional, where you will have to stand and deliver information in front of a group. It's great that you want to really develop those skills. It means that you realize the value in being able to talk in front of groups. It is a very good and employable skill.

After reading this book – and after you have collected all the tools and tricks you need – you'll be able to get up in front of any group and talk. That's all public speaking is when you think about it. It's just talking. It's just talking and people listening to you talk. That seems over-simplified but if you look at it in an over-simplified way then public speaking isn't such a big deal.

There is a lot of planning that goes into preparing to speak in public. Or at least there SHOULD BE a lot of preparing. This book will help you with all of the before, during and after that's involved.

If you follow the advice in this book, you will find yourself becoming quite a gifted orator. While you might not end up on the high paid lecture circuit – but then again maybe you will – at the very least you will gain enough confidence to make an important presentation at the office, emcee a dinner or even make a speech at a conference.

I've been speaking in front of groups of people – small, medium and large groups - since I was very young. It was scary at first, but the more I did it the more I grew as a speaker. The more I practiced, the more I learned. The same will happen for you.

This isn't a textbook, although I guess it could be used as one and I wouldn't discourage any college or high school from buying this book in great volume for their students. While this book does contain quotes and information from some very knowledgeable and experienced people, it is not research-heavy. That's not what you really want or need.

Public Speaking: Simple Steps to Improve Your Skills is a simple guide that will help make you a stronger, more confident public speaker.

Read on and enjoy!

According to most studies, people's number one fear is public speaking. Number two is death. Death is number two. Does that sound right? This means to the average person, if you go to a funeral, you're better off in the casket than doing the eulogy.
~ Jerry Seinfeld

You're not alone. Lots of people fear public speaking.

Lots of people are terrified of public speaking. They get nervous and start sweating. Their hands get clammy and their mouth gets dry. Their minds go blank.

They think, Oh man! What do I say? How do I say it? And in front of how many people?

What if I say something stupid? What if I forget to say anything, even if it is stupid?

What if the audience hates me? They might boo me off the stage. They'll throw stuff and chase me from the building waving pitchforks and burning torches. My name will be synonymous with epic failure!

What if I embarrass my family? They'll have to move out of town in disgrace. We'll have to change our name and enter the Speaker Protection Program. We'll be living in Idaho, purposely speaking in phony accents and wearing sunglasses everywhere we go for the rest of our lives.

We're starting to get off track here. There is no Speaker Protection Program that I know of any way, but you get the idea. However, here's a fact: Public speaking is frightening to lots of people. And you might be one of those people. If you are, that's okay because you are in good company.

So many people would rather do anything but get in front of a crowd and give a talk or some kind of presentation or speech. Even just standing up and introducing a guest speaker to a group petrifies people. Does this describe you? If it does, you don't need to worry because it's common.

Paul L. Witt, PhD, an assistant professor of communication studies at Texas Christian University, Fort Worth, believes speaking in public is one hurdle that some people just cannot clear.

"It is even scarier than rattlesnakes. The idea of making a presentation in public is the No. 1 fear reported by people in the U.S," Witt says (DeNoon, 2006).

I've never really been bothered by speaking in front of groups and have done it for as long as I can remember. When I was a kid growing up in Port Vue, Pennsylvania, I attended a Catholic elementary school. I wanted to be an altar boy when I was in third grade, but I didn't get chosen. It was a crushing blow for a little kid.

My teacher at the time, her name was Sister Timothy (no relation), asked me if I'd like to become a lector instead. In the Catholic Church, a lector is a person who reads some of the scripture aloud at mass. Sister told me that since I was a fairly good reader that learning to be a lector might be a good opportunity for me. So, I started reading in public beginning in the third grade, during Sunday masses and at masses during the week. I would stand up in front of a church filled with people and read. I'd read from the scripture. I'd read announcements from the bulletin. I didn't think much of it. At the time, I think

I was too young – and probably too naïve – to know enough to be scared.

Fast forward many years: I've worked as a radio and television news reporter. I've given countless presentations and emceed many events. I've hosted talk shows and interview programs. I believe my experiences as a young kid nudged me toward my profession. It possibly laid the groundwork.

However, even though I've been talking in front of crowds since I was young, that doesn't mean I don't get anxious sometimes and maybe a little apprehensive. It's a natural reaction but it is something people can and DO overcome.

So, maybe you share this same phobia with millions and millions of other Americans. That's okay. With preparation and persistence, you can clear this hurdle. I've learned a lot over the years and am glad to share the information with you.

The best way to overcome your fear of public speaking is to speak in public. Speak in public often. Speak in public every chance that you get. That's not to say you should stand on a crate at Costco and start gabbing. Approach this a little more strategically.

As you read through this book, I think – no, I KNOW – you will find that the tips and suggestions you will read in the following pages will help you a great deal.

You want to improve your public speaking skills and that's why you've bought this book.

So let's get to work!

Speech is power: speech is to persuade, to convert, to compel.
~ Ralph Waldo Emerson

Why being a good public speaker is important.

Why is it important to be a good public speaker? The answer to that question is obvious but keep reading anyway.

Just look at some really successful people and you will see that the vast majority of them were or are great public speakers. We can invoke names like Ronald Reagan, Bill Clinton and Steve Jobs. But what about that one guy at work who's really good at standing up at meetings, explaining himself fully and expressing his thoughts well?

You want to be like that guy.

The people who seem to succeed in their careers the most are the ones who communicate well. They speak well and they listen well. You really can't put a price on good speaking and communication skills.

When I was a young television reporter working in Dallas, Texas, I had the opportunity to attend a news conference hosted by Herb Kelleher, the founder of Southwest Airlines. He was probably one of the most dynamic individuals I've had the opportunity to cover during my time as a reporter.

During the news conference at Love Field in Dallas – where I think the topic was Southwest Airlines unveiling some new travel routes – Herb started talking about topics that had nothing to do with the news conference. One reporter asked Herb what he looked for most when hiring people and his response was really interesting. Herb said what he looks for most in people is good communication skills.

I will not try to quote Herb because my memory doesn't serve me well enough, but basically he said the most important skill he looked for in someone was how well they communicated. He said communication skills were the most important to him. His words stuck with me over the years.

So, why is it important to be a good public speaker? Well, other than what Mr. Kelleher stated, let's look at some other very good reasons:

-Self-Confidence: Having good public speaking skills boosts your self-confidence. You feel better about yourself. People feel better about you. Self-confidence is a good thing. We all can agree on that.

-Get more comfortable around others: This follows suit with self-confidence. People who show that they are comfortable around others are the type of people that others want to be around.

-Stand out in the crowd: Having self-confidence often leads to leadership roles which gives you the opportunity to prove yourself, which gives you the chance to advance at your job.

-Leadership: People who are good speakers and good communicators are often tapped for leadership roles in their communities.

-At some point in your life you're going to have to speak in public: So, why not get good at something that's very, very important, something that will give you confidence, and that will help you grow professionally and personally?

In my research before writing this book, I did not find any comments or evidence to the contrary regarding the importance of improving your public speaking skills. What we are talking about here is logical.

You will gain self-confidence by starting to speak in front of groups, small, medium and large (eventually). This will help you become more comfortable around other people. The more comfortable you are, the more self-confidence you gain. It's a good cycle.

Becoming a person who stands out from the rest of the crowd will really increase your chances of advancing professionally. Standing out can lead to you earning leadership positions, and that's a very good thing.

And finally, you're going to have to speak before people eventually any way. So, get good at it. The pros are there and it's pretty hard to come up with any cons.

So, as you begin exploring ways to improve your skills as a public speaker, remember that when you present in front of a group that you have to have a goal in mind. You have to have points you want to make.

You don't want to be known as the Pointless Presenter. You won't get asked to speak much if that's the case. You might not even get invited to many parties. You don't want to be the lonely, bad speaker. You want to be the well-liked, good speaker.

Read on and learn more on how to make that happen for you!

A wise man speaks because he has something to say, a fool speaks because he has to say something.
~ Plato

WHAT'S YOUR POINT?

Have you ever had the (mis)fortune of sitting in an audience while the speaker at the podium is droning on and on and making very little sense? You occasionally hear snippets of useful information that seem pertinent to the topic, but you feel like the speaker is all over the map. It is a frustrating experience for people on the listening end.

Please don't be that that type of person who is speaking. As you continue reading this section you will understand why you should not be that type of speaker and how you can avoid becoming that kind of speaker.

If you were taking a long trip, you would not travel without a trusty map or a GPS system. If you were going grocery shopping, you would not go without a detailed list. So, it just stands to reason that you would not make a speech or presentation without having a plan.

You don't want to be one of those speakers who, while you are talking and when you are finished, has audience members asking "What's your point?"

If they don't get your point that means you did a shabby job of presenting. And the main reason why that might have happened is that you went in without a road map or a shopping list. By that, I mean you went in without a plan. You didn't do a good job of mapping out what you wanted to say, or maybe you did no mapping at all.

The bottom line is that if you are going to give a speech, you have to know what you are going to say and how you are going to say it. Of course, this excludes those actors who didn't think they were going to win the Oscar, who then won the Oscar, and then went on babbling during their acceptance speech about how they never expected to win an Oscar. On second thought, while we probably can give those people a little break, they should have some sort of plan too.

While a few really gifted speakers can stand in front of a group and give an incredible off-the-cuff speech that really doesn't work for the average person. Have a plan. Work from an outline. If you don't have a fully written out speech, work from notes or note cards.

Speaker, coach and author Chris Witt is one of many experts who preaches that planning a speech and knowing the points you want to make *before* you begin talking will help you make those points clear to your audience.

"Identify your specific purpose: What do you want your audience *to do* as a result of hearing you speak? Be as precise as possible," says Witt (n.d.).

So as you are preparing your speech or presentation, ask yourself this question: what's the reaction i want from this audience?"

Do you just want to entertain them? Do you want to inform them? Do you want to motivate them to act in a certain way? And as you ask yourself these questions, work to make sure that the content of your presentation remains focused on the goal that you have in mind.

You don't want people in the audience asking "what's his point?"

I recently gave a presentation to a group of government administrators that was titled "how to prepare for media interviews." these people were in charge of both government and non-government agencies and they wanted to know how to best prepare themselves for being interviewed by a reporter. I narrowed my talk down to some specific scenarios, points and suggestions and didn't stray into any other content areas. My presentation was part of an all-day seminar and I was asked to focus on that one particular aspect. So, that's what i did.

In doing so, in the end people were not asking "what was his point?"

Here are some easy to follow steps to stay on-point with your presentation:

> -Identify the topic of your speech. Make sure that all aspects of your presentation point back to that topic. if not, you risk straying from your point.

-Identify the supporting points you want to make in your talk. It's usually three to five points depending on how long you are being asked to present. Stay focused on your content.

-Also focus on your audience. Make sure the information you are giving is pertinent to that audience and remains relevant.

-Stay succinct. Make sure you are clear and concise in your delivery and that you follow your "road map."

-Remain relevant throughout your talk. Your audience will thank you later and probably shower you with applause.

We have not reached the part of this book yet where we discuss exactly how to create the speech, whether to write it out word for word or use notes, or note cards. That will come later on. This section deals solely with staying on-point and i don't want you to catch me going off-point and straying from the topic at hand.

There is logic behind me stressing the importance of staying on topic during presentations. You don't want to lose your audience. You don't want audience members thinking you are scattered and can't focus. There's nothing that can prevent your spouse or children from thinking that. You'll have to get a different kind of help in that area from a different kind of book. However, you can hold onto your listeners by staying focused.

You cannot risk losing your audience. If you are unfocused, if audience members are asking each other "What's his/her point?" then you already have lost them.

The best way to keep your audience is to know your audience. In our next section, we will discuss the importance of knowing your audience before, during and after your presentation.

As you continue reading this book you are taking some positive steps toward getting better – and maybe even really good – at this public speaking thing. And when you get better – and then really, really good – just think of all the possibilities.

Be sincere; be brief; be seated.
~Franklin D. Roosevelt

Know your audience

There's a joke that legendary comedian Steve Martin does on his 1977 album "Let's Get Small" that really makes the point for this section. The setting is San Francisco. Before getting to the actual joke, Martin does a preamble where he admits he doesn't gear his material for a particular audience but he wants to make an exception because of a plumbers' convention in town.

His joke goes like this:

"This lawn supervisor was out on a sprinkler maintenance job and he started working on a Findlay sprinkler head with a Langstrom 7" gangly wrench. just then, this little apprentice leaned over and said, 'you can't work on a Findlay sprinkler head with a Langstrom 7"wrench.'well this infuriated the supervisor, so he went and got volume 14 of the Kinsley manual, and he reads to him and says, 'the Langstrom 7" wrench can be used with the Findlay sprocket.' just then, the little apprentice leaned over and said, 'it says sprocket not socket!'"

And then, Martin says "Were these plumbers supposed to be here at this show…?"

That joke always cracks me up. Of course, Martin made up the name of the wrench and the sprinkler system, but that is beside the point. The joke speaks to the message of this section, and it speaks loudly and clearly: KNOW YOUR AUDIENCE.

I have the opportunity to speak before all different kinds of groups: writers, teachers, school administrators, young people, older people, religious leaders, parents, business executives. One of the first things I do before preparing for any speech or presentation – and I suggest you do the same – is do some homework to understand who your audience is and what that audience expects.

Experts say that kind of homework is vital.

"When you know more about your audience and their expectations, you'll be able to tailor your talk to make it more interesting. Your audience will be engaged and satisfied, and you will willingly accept their applause at the end," says noted author and presenter Tom Ricci (2012).

So, how do you get to know your audience before you speak? The best thing to do is to ask questions of the organizers who invited you to talk. Here is a list of questions, in no particular order of importance:

-Are you speaking to a certain group or association?

-Is this a general audience?

-What's the average age of the group?

-What about gender and education level?

-Are the members of this group particularly conservative or liberal?

-Are there any language or cultural concerns?

-Is this presentation planned around a specific event, celebration or cause?

-What's likely on the audience's mind at the time you are speaking?

-How long are you supposed to speak?

-What are the general family circumstances such as marital status and children/grandchildren?

-How knowledgeable is the audience on the subject?

The point is that it's important that you must do your research before you start collecting your thoughts and composing your presentation. You don't want to under-inform anyone. You certainly don't want to offend anyone. In fact, the best way to ensure that you are going to give an awesome, spot-on speech is to take some time beforehand and ask a lot of questions.

You'll have to do your homework, especially if they expect you to know a thing or two about "the Langstrom 7!" but even if you don't know the difference between a sprocket and a socket, you can always take some time to learn a little first before diving in.

Ask a lot of pre-event questions. Use Google – or the search engine of your choice – to see if the organization has a website where you can learn more. I'm confident that would be an easy – and fun – step for you in this public speaking process.

So, the moral of this story – or at least this section – is that you should invest a little time beforehand asking questions and preparing. It doesn't take all that long to get to know your audience.

And as you make the time to know your audience, you also must make the time to ensure that you know your topic well. In our next section, we'll read about the importance of knowing your material. As was mentioned, you will be doing some research.

It's not about being a whole lot smarter than the people you will be addressing. It's about knowing what you need to know to entertain, impress and inform the audience that is looking forward to hearing you speak.

Say not always what you know, but always know what you say.
~ Claudius

Know your material

I don't "live by" many phrases or anecdotes but one I particularly like to say every once in a while is that "I am smart enough to know that I don't know enough." It's not very poetic and I haven't copyrighted it, so if that phrase appears in your next book at least cite me as a source. I'd appreciate it.

This section deals with facing the truth that you really need to know your material when you are preparing to speak before an organization or group. If you don't know your material and if you try to fake it, the audience will know and they won't appreciate it. Not knowing your material increases the odds that you won't get invited back and word might get around that you don't do your homework.

I was once asked to speak at a Minority Enterprise Development Conference and was flattered to receive the invitation. Admittedly, I was apprehensive because I didn't know much about the group or what they did. I was emceeing the event and even though I wasn't expect to say anything profound, I did need to know some things about the organization and what it did. I didn't want to come off as unprepared.

So, I did some homework. I learned about the organization and its mission to assist minority owned businesses and help them grow and thrive. I spoke with the organizers about what they do and asked if there were specific comments they wanted me to make. I sprinkled that information throughout my comments, said a few humorous things throughout the night and in the end, the evening was successful. And I was invited back several more times to speak to the group. That's a good feeling when you're invited back to speak to the same organization. It's validation of your work.

My goal that first evening of speaking at the Minority Enterprise Development Conference was to let the audience know that I knew a little about them and they appreciated that. I did my best to NOT pretend that I was an expert on the organization. Doing so would have been a mistake.

According to Susan Tardanico, CEO and founding partner of the authentic leadership alliance, not knowing your material and trying to prove how smart you are to your audience will not work in your favor.

"By trying to impress your audience with your intellect, you create more distance and could come across as arrogant," says Tardanico (2012).

Her point is that you don't want to come off as a wise guy. You want to come off as the nice guy (or gal) who cares enough to learn a little about the group.

So, what's the best approach here? It's pretty simple:

-Ask questions of the organizers who know a lot about the group. They can add some insight to your comments and this will help a great deal.

-Find out exactly who it is that you'll be speaking to just to make sure you have the right demographics: age, gender and all those other important factors.

-Log onto the Web and research the group you are speaking to and the subject you are being asked to speak about. Chances are they are asking you to pontificate about a topic you already know, but don't take any chances.

-Ask how long they want you to speak. If they are expecting just ten minutes but you've prepared for thirty minutes then you will have a problem.

-Write down six to ten general ideas that you want to cover in your remarks. You'll use six for a shorter speech and ten for a longer one, of course.

-Make sure you know enough about each point to show how much you care enough to do the research.

-Write down your thoughts, either on paper or on note cards. (We will talk more about this at greater length later on in the book.)

-Figure out what you want to say at the beginning and at the end. Start strong and finish strong.

-Go over your remarks many, many times before you actually present. (We will dedicate a whole section to practicing too, but there's no reason why we can't mention that important part several times.)

Now consider this: When I say "know your material" that means several things. That means know important facts about the organization or group that you will be speaking to. That also means know who they are, what they do and why they do it. I don't mean memorize the information because you could end up sounding robotic, or you might get frustrated. I mean be really familiar with your information. The more familiar you are, the better you know your stuff, and the better you will perform as a presenter.

At this point, you might have noticed that I keep referencing groups that have invited you to speak. However, no one has invited you anywhere to do any kind of speaking just yet. We will address that later on because there are ways to get invited to speak and there are ways to invite yourself too, in a non-egotistical way.

I'm hoping everything we've covered in this section makes sense to you.

In the next section, we will discuss what it means to know the room. Knowing the room means several things, which you will find out as you read on!

You can speak well if your tongue can deliver
the message of your heart.
~ John Ford

Know the room

I often have the opportunity to facilitate writing seminars at local writing conferences. It's always a lot of fun to work with people who are in various stages of writing projects. I love working with other writers and helping them with their writing.

During these workshops and seminars, I always have participants go through a series of writing exercises to get their thoughts flowing and get them working together. I have a small collection of writing exercises that I like to use. In one exercise, I have participants huddle together in small groups where they take turns interviewing each other and writing descriptive bios of each other. This exercise works best when the room is configured with movable desks and chairs.

A few years ago, I was scheduled to facilitate a writing workshop and decided beforehand to use the bio exercise. It turned out to be a mistake. The room we were assigned to had desks and chairs bolted to the floor and there was no way the bio exercise would work because the participants could not collaborate in small groups. I had to punt and use another exercise that wasn't nearly as fun.

I didn't make the time to "know the room." I didn't know how the place was configured and that forced me to redirect everything I did. That happened because I didn't out in the time before we started and it threw me off track.

There was another time when I didn't do my room homework and it cost me some money. At least, I believe it did. I was invited to host a book signing at a local bookstore and I was excited about that. Book signings can be fun and entertaining. But they also can be depressing for the author when few people show up.

Prior to the event, I spoke with the store's community relations person and was told I would have a small table in the café area where I could sit, talk with customers, and sign piles of books for sale. (I made up the selling of piles of books but you get the idea.)

There also was going to be a small podium set up on the table that I could use to present and answer questions from the throngs of people standing in line to buy my book. (I made up the throngs part too. There were a handful of people there, at best.)

Again, I didn't take the time to learn the room set-up and the event did not turn out well. The table and podium were there but were tucked away in a far off corner of the café. And there was no microphone. I was off in a corner in a crowded café with a stack of books and a small podium with no microphone. People could not hear me or notice me. The event was a flop.

I didn't make more of an effort to "know the room" so potential book buyers didn't even know that I was there. In addition, there was a lot of competition for attention that evening. It was Teacher's Night where local educators got discounts on materials. The store had "special" signs everywhere and teachers were flocking to the specials like bees to a hive. With the exception of a few small signs, people didn't know I was there.

I should have planned ahead. I should have asked more questions about the set up. I should have asked to be placed closer to the center of the café. I should have asked for a microphone to make a brief presentation. I should have asked if there were other events scheduled for that evening.

You have to know more about the environment where you will speak or present. So, how can you "know the room" before your presentation?

Here are some things you can ask your contact:

-Is the room where I will be speaking a large room or a small room?

-Will the size of the room allow for participant interaction? Or will it be too big?

-Is the room bright, or is there "mood lighting"?

-Will I have to project my voice and speak loudly or speak in a normal tone?

-Is there a microphone, and what type? Is it stationary or wireless?

-Will there be competition for attention?

-What's the room configuration? Is it theater seating or classroom style?

-Does the room allow for group exercises or audience participation?

-Will I be standing or sitting? Or both?

-Can I move around when I speak?

As you can see, there are a few things you need to ask in order to know the room. You might think some of the above questions don't matter but if you are planning an intimate talk and end up in a larger setting and that could throw off your plans.

You could be expecting a microphone with a podium where you can place your written speech or notes and then find out you have neither. That could throw you off course as well.

You want to be as comfortable as possible and you won't be as comfortable as possible if the room where you will be speaking is a completely different environment from what you will be expecting.

All you need to do is ask a few simple questions first.

In our next section, we will delve into a topic that's simple and one you've probably heard before at some time in your life. It's an old rule to follow when it comes to public speaking and it works every time.

Happy continued reading!

Be still when you have nothing to say; when genuine passion moves you, say what you've got to say, and say it hot.
~ D. H. Lawrence

Tell them what you are going to tell them.

    People like structure. They like order. They like to know what to expect. I'm that way. You might be the same way too.

    There's comfort in knowing what lies ahead. Surprises are great, when it comes to birthday parties or holiday presents. But in other facets of our lives, surprises can be a little unsettling sometimes.

    That leads me to say this: for the most part, audiences like to know what to expect. While they like surprising aspects of a story, some twists and turns, they do like to know what they are getting from their speakers.

When someone is going to an event with a guest speaker, they know that person is going to address a certain topic. But that's not exactly what I mean. If you're going to an event where an astronaut is the guest speaker you can be pretty sure that he or she is going to talk about space travel, or some related topic. But it's not really the topic that is of concern here; it's the delivery of that topic.

If you pay close attention to some of the best speakers out there you will find that they follow a very simple, tried but true rule:

-Tell them what you are going to tell them. Tell them. Tell them what you just told them.

Some of you might think, ell that's really redundant. But time and again, this approach to public speaking works. John Baldoni, president of Baldoni Consulting, believes audience members find comfort in this old practice.

"Giving listeners structure gives people an opportunity to shape not only what you say but what you intend," insists Baldoni (2012).

Why is structure important? Because people like it. Research that I've done has traced this method all the way back to Aristotle. That's how time-tested and reliable this presentation method is when speaking to people.

I've used this method over and over during the years and it does help. It helps me organize my thoughts and it lets the listeners know what to expect.

Let's say you are giving a talk about a fictional company called acme widgets. Let's say that you work for this company and it's your job to explain why the widget industry is important. (Remember that a widget really isn't a thing. it's a name people give to small gadgets that won't really have a name.) So, here's how you would apply this "tell them" approach:

"Good evening, everyone. My name is Adam Zapple and I am here tonight to tell you about all of the great things going on in the widget industry. I will give a little history on the evolution of the widget. I also will be discussing how widgets are the driving force behind the economy. Then, I will tell you why you should consider a career in the growing widget industry because the widget will be the focal point of our economy someday."

As you can see, in that opening paragraph Mr. Zapple laid out a road map that both he and his listeners can follow. In the opening, he tells listeners that he will tell them all the great things going on in the world of widgets. He is letting people know "Okay folks, here's where I am going with my talk."

After offering the overview, Mr. Zapple proceeds to let people know the details and special areas on which he will focus his presentation. That's what you should do when starting a presentation or speech, at least one of some length. Moving on from there, Mr. Zapple promises to discuss how widgets are the backbone of our economy. That's exciting and new information. And then he moves on to let people know they might have a future in widgets. This is all great stuff and keeps the audience riveted.

Now, assume that Mr. Zapple has kept all of his promises and touched on all of these topics. How would he then "tell them what he just told them"? Basically he would summarize:

"In closing, I would like to say that I hope you learned some interesting things about the widget industry. We talked about how the widget evolved from a tiny component to the significant device it is today. We also learned how widgets came to be a big item of interest on the New York stock exchange and how it contributes so much to our nation's economy and makes it strong. And finally, I hope that i have opened your eyes to all the possible opportunities you might find in this wonderful industry. Who knows? There might be a widget in your future. Again, my name is Adam Zapple and it has been a great pleasure to speak to you this evening. Have a safe trip home."

(Cue the thunderous applause!)

This is a good pattern to follow if you are going to speak or give a presentation. Let the listeners know what to expect and then in the end let them know why what you told them is significant. By doing this you are reinforcing your message. Doing that helps your message stick a little longer and stronger.

After you have finished reading this section, I suggest you go on Google – or the search engine of your choice - and search for "tell them. Tell them what you are going to tell them. Tell them what you told them." you will find a lot of information on this tried and true speaking technique.

Remember, people like structure. They like order. They like to know what to expect. This makes sense and it works.

Also remember that your goal is to be a public speaker who offers every audience meaningful and memorable information. You can do this and you are taking steps toward that goal.

In our next section, we will explore a simple topic. Actually, what I really should say it that we will be focusing on the actual word "simple." As in keeping your presentation simple. You want to inform and not confuse. Our next section will help you with that.

No one can remember more than three points.
~ Philip Crosby

KEEP IT SIMPLE

How many times have you sat through a speech and then tried to recall as much as possible about what the speaker shared with the group? Did you find that challenging? Try it the next time you attend a presentation. Don't take notes and don't record the talk. Just sit there and pay attention. Really pay attention. What you will find is that unless you have a freakishly good memory you only will remember some of what you heard.

If that's the case, don't feel badly about yourself. That's the way most people's minds work. There's only so much space on the hard drive.

Don't be discouraged by the fact that people won't remember everything you tell them during a speech or presentation. It's normal. In fact, many studies show that audience members will only remember about a third, or less, of what you tell them. That's a little depressing but that shows why it's important to make sure that when making a speech or presentation that you need to keep it simple.

Nick Morgan, a Forbes Magazine contributor and author of *Trust Me: Four Steps to Authenticity and Charisma* suggests that simple speeches are the best kinds of speeches. He also insists that speeches are not necessarily the best way to transmit information. According to Morgan, "Speeches are an inefficient form of communication. People don't remember much of what they hear, so focus and keep it simple" (Smith, 2013).

Yes, speeches are inefficient. A lot of the information gets lost during the transmission. People in the audience let their minds wander. They check their phones for messages. They answer some texts. They check the scores of the baseball game. They play Candy Crush. They invite others to play Candy Crush. They post on Facebook that they are at a boring speech, which gets a bunch of "likes" before the speech is even over.

Why do listeners struggle to pay attention during presentations? It's mainly because the speaker isn't getting his or her message across very well. They aren't receiving the message because the presenter is not presenting the message well.

Let's pause for a moment. This is not to say that even the most inspiring of speakers doesn't lose an audience member or two to "runaway brain" every now and then. I am sure that Steve Jobs lost some listeners occasionally. My point is that if you keep your speech simple and you keep the message simple that you simply will have a better chance of connecting with your audience. And you will have a better chance of your information sticking with your audience.

Here is a list of tips of things to keep in mind as you work to "keep it simple" in your presentation:

-Be prepared. Practice to get it right.

-Relax.

-Use direct language.

-Speak clearly and pronounce your words properly.

-Don't use a $5 word when a 5-cent word will do.

-Avoid acronyms or confusing jargon.

-Come up with three to five main points you want to cover and stick to them.

-Tell a story with a beginning, middle and end.

-Stick to your topic. Don't stray.

If you are told you have ten minutes to speak, finish in less than ten minutes.

If you take a look at this list you will see that each of these suggestions makes sense in your quest to keep your presentation simple.

You also should keep in mind that if you are tackling a complex topic in your talk that you will have to take extra care in simplifying your presentation. Remember, just because you understand a topic that does not mean that the average person in the audience will understand it.

For example, if your expertise is finance and you are giving a talk on how to make the best investments to lower your tax rate you should take great steps to simplify the information you are relaying to your audience. To be honest, that kind of information makes my head swim. So, unless the presenter simplifies the information, I will be lost. Just because it's clear to you does not mean it'll be clear to the average person.

Later on in this book, we will focus a little more closely on some of the tips mentioned in the list above and get into a little more detail. But this list is pretty straightforward. And it is simple too!

If you think about it, simplifying your information is something that you will be able to do pretty easily. Use as your motivation the fact that you don't want to lose any of your listeners. While you know people are not going to be paying attention 100% of the time, you still want to improve your chances.

Imagine how well you will do when you break things down and simplify your speech. In fact, keep your imagination going because in the next section we will discuss how you can put yourself in the right frame of mind and see yourself giving a knockout performance even before you step up to the podium.

Talk low, talk slow, and don't talk too much.
~ John Wayne

Imagine yourself giving a really, really good speech

It sounds kind of corny – and maybe even Disney-like – to say this but if you visualize yourself giving a good speech before you actually give your speech that it will help you a little bit. It won't improve the content of your presentation, and it won't guarantee that your listeners will hang on every word, but it will at least make you feel a little more relaxed as your moment in the spotlight approaches.

Here are a few of the things I do when preparing for a presentation. As I go over my notes, or my script, I make mental notes of when to look up at the audience and when to try and engage the listeners. I look for spots where I might be able to toss in a humorous comment, and I even let my mind wander to imagine whether people might find that comment as humorous as I do. Sometimes the imaginary people do and sometimes they don't.

I think about the room and the people inside it and I look for spots where I might make a good connection with the people there. It might sound a little strange, but it works for me.

What I do is visualize the process of what I am doing and it helps me. Does my approach make me a better speaker? Well, I can say that it does make me feel more prepared and relaxed. It makes me less anxious, and even though I've done a lot of presentations, I still do get a little anxious occasionally.

The thing is that if you look and act anxious behind the podium, your audience will know. If they know you are nervous, they will focus more on that than what you are trying to tell them. Richard Zeoli, author of the *7 Principles of Public Speaking*, says an uncomfortable speaker creates an uncomfortable audience.

"People want to listen to someone who is interesting, relaxed, and comfortable. In the routine conversations we have every day, we have no problem being ourselves. Yet too often, when we stand up to give a speech, something changes," says Zeoli (2014).

Yes, things do change. When we stand behind the podium, we are still ourselves but someone else at the same time. For those of you who are reluctant public speakers, this can seem like an out of body experience. You don't want to be that uncomfortable presenter, but with preparation – and visualization can be part of the preparation – you can become more relaxed. When you become more relaxed you can more easily improve your public speaking skills.

I am sure you have heard someone give this public speaking advice: In order to help calm yourself down, look out into the audience and imagine the folks in front of you in their underwear. I don't know who came up with that recommendation but I cannot think of anything more distracting that thinking of a bunch of underwear clad people in front of me. And what if you see someone in the front row that you find attractive? What will happen to your concentration then? Would that make you less nervous or more nervous?

So, what are some things that you can do to help you with the visualization process? Here are some suggestions:

-Visualize your goal, which is giving a really great presentation.

-Picture that in your mind.

-Start developing a positive attitude that your presentation will be a good one.

-Concentrate on your task of developing good material but be realistic in knowing that not everything you say will be a gem. Be honest with yourself.

-Envision the people who will be hearing your speech (Fully clothed!). Think of people smiling at the right times and looking concerned at the right times.

-Keep telling yourself that your presentation will go well because you are preparing properly.

-Be realistic and admit you will likely make some mistakes. You might flub a line or lose your place momentarily. Recognize the truth that your talk won't be perfect and accept that.

-See yourself at the podium and see that you are in control.

-Make a "mental video" of you speaking and see how calm and collected you are at that moment.

Also remember the importance of pausing and taking a deep breath as you are staring your visualization. It will help you relax.

I understand if you don't think you can buy into the visualization approach. It doesn't work for everyone, but it helps me. I suggest you give it a try before you decide whether or not it's for you.

So, as we recap this section just keep in mind all of these simple suggestions. Collectively, they all look like parts of a positive thinking program. Actually, that's what visualization is any way.

However, keep in mind as you are visualizing throughout this process, you can't focus on all of the good things that will make you feel warm and fuzzy inside. You can imagine a wonderful speech, followed by thunderous applause, followed by an invitation to return and speak again. But visualization also involves thinking about things that might or could go wrong.

If anything does go wrong, how will you react? What will you do to fix the situation? I don't mention this part to freak you out. I mention it because it is part of the overall preparation. Think about "Plan B".

If people don't laugh at that first humorous anecdote, how will you move on? If the audience isn't interested in doing a little interaction, what can you do to get the listeners interested? It's like driving somewhere and needing to have an alternate route just in case. Having that alternate route will help you relax even more which will contribute to an even stronger presentation.

Something else that contributes to the success of a speech or presentation is your overall demeanor and that's what we will discuss in our next chapter.

Read on. We're about to get happy!

The human brain starts working the moment you are born and never stops until you stand up to speak in public.
~ George Jessel

Be happy to be there

As we've established and as you already know, speaking in front of groups can be pretty unnerving for many people. People who are unnerved often show their feelings on their face and by their mannerisms. When they do that, they look less than happy to be there and present information to the group. You need to project a happy and positive attitude.

Author Ron Clendenin (n.d.) insists that speakers who show that they are happy to be where they are at the time of their presentations connect with their audiences: "You can almost always smile, even in a serious speech. It will always facilitate a connection with your audience. Your smile invites your audience to join your positive and happy energy."

Smiling when you don't feel like it or when things aren't necessarily going your way is not easy. But you can do it. Here's a simple public speaking tip that maybe isn't as simple as it seems: Just be happy to be there. Or at least do your best to show that you are happy to be there.

For example, if you've been invited to emcee an awards dinner do you think you will come off well if you act like Debbie Downer? For those of you unfamiliar with Debbie, she was a recurring character on Saturday Night Live for many years. The immensely talented and funny actress Rachel Dratch played Debbie, a character who was always the bearer of bad news and negative feelings.

At this point, I *should* suggest that you take a reading break, log onto YouTube and search for Debbie Downer clips. However, if I did that you would not keep reading this section. So, please keep reading. (Okay, I know you're going to watch YouTube clips now. I'll see you soon.)

Welcome back!

As you probably saw, Debbie could vacuum the happiness and positivity out of any gathering. That's not the type of speaker and presenter you want to be because you will just bring people down. When you are invited to present somewhere – whether it's at a work function or before a few hundred people at your local community center – you have to set all of your negative feelings aside and do your job as a presenter. People are expecting you to do a good job. In fact, they are pulling for you. (We will address this topic in more detail later.)

In spite of what you might be feeling at the moment, focus on the task of being the best, most entertaining and informative presenter that you can be. You can do this.

The hardest talk I ever gave was at my mother's funeral. As you can imagine, and maybe this type of situation has happened to you, I really was not in the mood to speak but I felt I owed it to her and our family. Mom battled Alzheimer's for many years and the disease robbed her of everything, especially her fun and witty personality. And that's what I talked about from the lectern in church.

It was a sad occasion, of course, but I took a few deep breaths, focused and shared some funny stories about Mom. It was in no way fun, but I did it. In spite of the circumstances, I was happy to be there to retell funny stories about my mother and celebrate her life.

These are the kinds of things you can do too. When you are called upon to present at a time when it might be one of the last things you want to do, please keep the following things in mind:

-Acknowledge the problem(s) you are facing at the moment, but focus on the task at hand. Remember that the audience is depending on you.

-Know that you can set aside your problems for a short while.

-Let go of that inner (or outer) conflict.

-Remember that the bad stuff isn't permanent.

-Tell yourself "I can do this."

-Do it.

There are going to be times when you have so much on your mind that you'd rather just sit on the couch with a cup of coffee and stare out the window than give a speech or presentation. Yet, you might not have a choice. Plus if you pass on that opportunity, it might not come around again, as in the case of me speaking at my mother's funeral.

So, as a short recap of this section consider this: There are going to be times when you have to present but don't want to present. Do it anyway. Recognize that you are facing some challenges and that you aren't feeling "up to it" but move forward. Think positively and tell yourself that you can do this. You will be amazed at what you can do in these situations.

Thanks for reading this section and allowing me to share a very personal story. I appreciate it. In our next section, we are going to discuss ways to overcome the nervousness you might encounter as you are approaching the podium.

Best way to conquer stage fright is to know
what you're talking about.
~ Michael H Mescon

Calm down. No one's going to hurt you.

Some people don't like it when others tell them to calm down. I am not sure if you are one of those people but I apologize in advance for saying that to you. Understand that in polite society today, we have gone past the time of throwing rotten fruit and vegetables at performers. When you are behind the podium and holding that microphone you have to keep telling yourself "This will be fine. Besides, no one is going to hurt me."

At least they shouldn't hurt you. I'm just kidding. Of course, they won't hurt you.

Please realize that while public speaking might make you uneasy and kind of queasy, it is a hurdle that you really need to clear in order for you to grow both professionally and personally.

Occasionally, I still get butterflies before presentations, so I'm a little familiar with public speaking apprehension. I understand it and I also understand that if you show your nervousness, your audience will pick up on it. Have you ever gone to a presentation and noticed that the person behind the podium seems so petrified that it's making you uncomfortable? You don't want to be that kind of speaker.

If you look and act anxious behind the podium, your audience will know. If they know you are nervous, they will focus more on that than what you are trying to tell them. You don't want that to happen, whether you are in front of a large crowd or an intimate one.

Here are some suggestions on how you can calm down and deliver a good presentation:

-Be prepared and know your material.

-Use the restroom before you start. One of the last things you want is that kind of distraction.

-Accept nervousness as part of the deal. Use the Force Luke! *(That's a quick Star Wars reference for any of you fans out there.)*

-Take a really deep breath.

-Take a drink of water.

-Relax your body. Don't be tense.

-Use your notes. (Later on we will talk about the benefit of using notes versus a full text script.)

-Visualize you enjoying yourself and giving a good speech.

-Like your audience and they will return the favor.

-Realize the speech won't be perfect and be okay with that.

-Know that the people in the audience want you to do well. Plus, they are NOT going to hurt you.

-Take another really deep breath because you are finished. Great job!

-Know that this presentation you just gave is one more to add to your collection.

One more piece of advice here: please do not drink alcohol or use any kind of mood altering substance before a speech. Ever. While some people might think alcohol will lubricate their brain and help them relax, it really is not helpful. Have you ever been to an event where someone speaking before the group has obviously been drinking? How would you rate that person's performance? How would you think of that speaker as a person knowing that he or she got in front of a gathering while three sheets to the wind, as my mother used to say?

As we recap, please remember the following: Come to your presentation ready and prepared. Use the restroom before stepping up to the microphone. Take a deep breath and take a sip of water. Work off of your notes or script fully knowing you won't be perfect. That's okay. No one is perfect. Finally, remember that no one is going to harm you. That is one fear you can set aside.

Keep in mind that the more relaxed you are the better you will feel. The better you feel; the better your presentation. Also know going in – as I have mentioned before – knowing that the people seated in the audience want to like you and you can use that to your advantage.

Read on and we will talk more about that in the next section.

There are only two types of speakers in the world. 1. The nervous and 2. Liars.
~ Mark Twain

The people listening want to like you.

You're mother probably told you at one time or another that not everyone you meet is going to be your friend. That's just something we all have to accept as a fact of life. But while that is true what you have to keep in mind is that the people in your audience – at least most of them – really want you to do well during your speech.

As we discussed earlier, people do not want to sit in an audience and watch an uncomfortable presenter stumble and quake through a presentation. The people in your audience really want to hear what you have to say and they want you to be really good at saying it.

The vast majority of your listeners are on your side even before to get in front of them. There is the occasional skeptic who will sit there with arms folded and snarled lip and seem to disagree with everything you say. There's no way around it and you have to accept that. Grouchy people are part of any group. As I said, not everyone you meet is going to be your friend.

Not long ago, I was serving as emcee for an awards event honoring teachers. It was a pretty large room holding maybe 500 people. When I emcee, my eyes are always surveying the crowd because I like to look people in the eyes – even in large groups – to make connections. During this particular event, there was one man close by who did not seem impressed with anything I said. His body language told me so.

At one point, I was sharing a quick story about my wife, who is a kindergarten teacher. One of her students that year had a real fixation with for turtles and tortoises. I jokingly mentioned that even I often got confused over the differences between turtles and tortoises. That little joke got a laugh, except from THAT one guy.

After the event, he came up to me and said (smugly), "Hey, turtles live in aquatic environments. Tortoises live on land. I can't believe you don't know that."

Yes, what he said was kind of rude and unnecessary.

I looked at him with a half-smile and said "Yes, I know. I was making a joke." Then the rude man walked away. Hopefully, he felt like a jerk.

My point is that except for that one guy, I am going to assume the majority of people in the audience liked the job that I did. That's the way you have to approach your presentations. You have to go in thinking that the people there in the group really want to like you.

People in any audience – or at least the normal and nice people – are rooting for you and don't want you to fail. According to David Brooks (n.d.) from Toastmasters International: "Most people hope for a good performance, most people are inherently on your side from the start. Therefore, even in an audience of strangers, most will be allies, not adversaries. Take comfort in their support."

Yes, take comfort in their support. Their support should give you confidence. That confidence will relax you and make you a better speaker.

Here are some ways to help make sure the audience likes you:

-Be friendly, welcoming and smile. You can even smile a little if you are touching on a serious subject.

-Show that you are well-versed in your topic and display confidence but not cockiness.

-Be authentic and real.

-Speak plainly and clearly. Remember how we mentioned earlier to avoid the super-big words when regular ones will suffice.

-Show that you are enjoying yourself.

-Be relevant and stay on topic.

-Work to engage the audience so that they feel a part of your presentation. (We will expound on this a little more later on.)

-Use humor when appropriate. (We will expound more on this one too.)

-Be a good storyteller.

-Follow all of the tips in this book. That will help you.

-Remember that not everyone is going to like you. Accept that and forge ahead.

These are all common sense suggestions. You need to be open, honest and sincere with your audience.

People can tell a phony when they see one. Have you ever gone to a presentation and seen a speaker who is trying too hard to be energetic and happy? Have you ever watched a speaker force the humor and the earnestness a bit too much to the point that you decide you don't like that person? The moment you as a listener reach that conclusion you stop listening. You decide the speaker doesn't have credibility and you are not buying into what he or she is selling. The presenter lost you. You don't want to be that type of speaker.

Be sincere. Be yourself. Be open and personal. That's what we are focusing on in the next section, being person and sincere. It works. Read on, please!

There are certain things in which mediocrity is not to be endured, such as poetry, music, painting, and public speaking.
~ Jean de la Bruyere

Use personal stories

Personal stories get people's attention. Just giving out a bunch of facts will not hold someone's attention unless you are giving an exam after the presentation. If you are standing before a group and just spitting out facts you might as well be reading from the phone book. Doing so increases the chances of you losing your audience. You don't want that to happen.

Personal stories work really, really well during presentations. People will identify with you more if you show some vulnerability and give them a little insight into your soul. You might be the kind of person who is reluctant to open up. If so, you have to overcome being reluctant if you want to become a successful presenter.

People like stories. Actually, people love stories, the personal kind. If you are giving a speech, people will like hearing personal stories about you. Not necessarily boastful stories about when you hit the game winning grand slam or stuck the landing for a perfect score. Make your stories real. Public speaking expert Chris Witt advises speakers to not make themselves the hero.

"There's a dilemma here. On the one hand, because stories — and personal stories, in particular — have so much power, you can strengthen just about any speech by telling a story (or two). And on the other hand, precisely because personal stories are so powerful, you have to be careful," Witt says (2013).

I recently had the privilege of emceeing an awards banquet for a writer's association in my area. I was flattered the organizers asked me. When you emcee any event – like an awards program – you offer some welcoming remarks, announce the award winners, make some (hopefully) humorous and clever remarks during the event, and then end the evening by thanking everyone for inviting you.

Emceeing these events is a lot of fun and I hope you have the opportunity to do this because you will enjoy yourself, and it's a great opportunity to speak while thinking on your feet. That is a useful skill to develop because it will help you both personally and professionally.

At the beginning of my opening remarks at this event, I shared a story about the business of writing that I knew the attendees there could identify with because they all have experienced – and currently experience – the highs and lows of trying to make it as a writer.

I told the group that I believe one of the greatest feelings a writer can have is going into a random bookstore they had never visited and seeing one of his or her books on a shelf. The people in the audience smiled and nodded. They identified with that. I told them that was what happened to me. I told the story about the time I walked into a random bookstore and on one of the shelves was a copy of my first book. I had never held a book signing at this store and never met the manager. Wow! They had my book in their store. That was a great feeling... but it disappeared quickly.

I told the group that what sucks the air out of that euphoric feeling of seeing one of your books in a random store is when that book is on the $1 bookshelf, which is the dumping ground for unsold books that managers are trying to unload. It's the Bermuda Triangle of unwanted inventory. That's where I found my book in that store. Again, audience members smiled and started laughing. They identified even more.

Then I added more to the story that amplified my pain. My book was on the $1 shelf and I wanted to buy it to save myself some embarrassment; however, I don't even have $1 in my wallet to buy my own lonesome book! The listeners laughed even more. Sure they laughed at my expense, but that's fine because he created a stronger connection with the group.

I closed my story by saying that I then left my lonely book on the shelf because I didn't want to use my ATM card to rescue. The clerk would have seen my name on the card, would have seen my name on the book, and then put two and two together. Wouldn't I have looked like a pathetic person? The people in the audience laughed. They could associate with my dilemma and appreciated that I shared it with them. I opened up with a personal story about personal failure and they liked it. The story worked.

So, when you are giving a speech and sharing a personal story make sure your story has a point, a purpose and is pertinent. Otherwise, you've lost your listeners and you won't be invited back to speak.

People enjoy hearing about personal stuff and you should make an effort to share those kinds of stories because they will help you relax and they also will help ease the tension. Personal stories reveal your "human" side.

In case you were wondering what types of stories you could possibly share with listeners:

-Specific aspects about your home life.

-Specific aspects about your professional life.

-Unusual experiences you've had in your life.

-Famous people you have met.

-Everyday people you've met who are impressive.

-Experiences you've had dealing with a particular personal challenge.

-Describing what special skills you might possess.

-Describing what special skills someone you know might possess.

-Stories of great personal triumph.

-Stories of great personal failure.

You might be thinking "What could I possibly have to share?" Please know that you are a more interesting person than you realize. You have some good stories to share and when you are presenting, the people in the crowd want you to share those stories with them. Give yourself more credit. You are an interesting person and likely have some interesting stories to share. Just follow the list of personal story ideas you see above and you will be able to come up with some good personal story material.

The moral of this story is that people like hearing personal stories. Those stories break down barriers and show that you are warm and real. People like that. People also like hearing funny stories and that's something we will address in the next section.

Once you get people laughing, they're listening
and you can tell them almost anything.
~ Herbert Gardner

Use humor

People like to laugh. If you do a Web search, you'll find a lot of information about the benefits of laughter. Just think about it. Don't you feel better after a good laugh? Some of the best public speakers are the ones who can skillfully weave humor into their presentations. I have found that audiences really enjoy a speaker who has a good sense of humor, but one who doesn't overdo it.

One of the most entertaining speakers I have ever had the pleasure of seeing is someone you would not think of as a humorist. I am talking about Brian Williams, the evening anchor for NBC Nightly News. A few years ago, he was the commencement speaker at my oldest son's college graduation. Williams was an amazing and entertaining speaker. It would not do him justice to say he was funny. He was hilarious, but at the appropriate times. While he did touch on some serious subjects, he mixed in the right amount of humor to keep the audience entertained, interested and informed.

Keep in mind that humor is not appropriate in every situation, but a sprinkling here and there is good. Humor helps ease the tension in the audience and helps the speaker too. Of course, you have to know when to crack a joke and when to play it straight. You develop a better sense of that over time. In the beginning, you have to use your instincts and common sense as to when to say something funny.

I try to sprinkle humor throughout presentations that I give. Most of it is spontaneous and unrehearsed. Those types of remarks seem to work best. In most cases, the rehearsed jokes seem... well, they seem rehearsed.

For example, a few years ago I was emceeing an awards banquet honoring some of the area's top decorated teachers. It was a fun event and people were having a good time. I introduced one of the award-winning teachers to say a few remarks. She stepped up to the podium, turned her back to the audience, and turned around wearing sunglasses and an oversized ball cap pulled to one side of her head. This teacher, a woman somewhere in her 40s, began to perform this really funny rap song that she wrote about the joys of being a teacher. To say the least, the crowd went crazy over this teacher's performance.

When it came to my turn again, I was thinking of something to say to acknowledge this teacher's great performance. So, I said something like "And for all of you education rap fans, Mrs. Smith will be performing next week at the downtown arena with Kanye and Lil' Bow Wow." The audience laughed some more and we moved on.

Listeners prefer spur-of-the-moment amusing comments as opposed to well-rehearsed and maybe even over-rehearsed jokes. At least, that's what my experience tells me. Those speakers who try to be exceedingly funny can alienate an audience.

Remember that a little humor goes a long way during a presentation. Chances are that you are not on the level of Jimmy Fallon or Ellen Degeneres, but you still have a sense of humor and can make people chuckle a little. Laughter loosens up an audience.

Toastmasters International's Joe Cooke insists that a little laughter goes a long way in a speech. According to Cooke (n.d.): "You don't have to elicit a roar of laughter from your audience. Sometimes a witty observation will produce no more than a smile or a twinkle in someone's eye. That's enough."

I agree with Cooke. A little bit of humor is enough.

A few years ago, I attended a workshop designed for people who wanted to sharpen their public speaking and presentation skills. The workshop offered several sessions and I attended one that focused on adding humor to presentations. However, I was really disappointed in the speaker. While he attempted to instruct listeners on the benefits of using humor in talks what he really was doing was testing out new comedy material. It seems he was an aspiring stand-up comedian who was hired to work as a presenter for this conference.

I spoke with some of my fellow attendees after the "comic's" presentation. We all felt the same way: we didn't learn much from him. As I said earlier, a little humor goes a long way.

So, how do you add humor to your presentation without turning off your audience? Here are some suggestions:

-Try to avoid opening your talk with a canned joke – the type you might find from doing a Google search - because if it's a bad joke, the rest of your presentation could go downhill.

-However, opening your talk with a humorous personal anecdote will help both you and the listeners relax and settle in.

-Poke fun at yourself. A little self-deprecating humor is very disarming.

-Exaggerated – but not totally outlandish – stories work well.

-Add pertinent humor. Jokes for the sake of jokes won't serve you well.

-Keep it clean. No off-color, crass or inappropriate jokes, please. And no bad language either.

-Sarcasm is fine as long as your audience realizes you are using sarcasm. Mockery can sometimes be misinterpreted.

-Watch some good speakers that you admire and see how they add humor to their talks.

-Keep the humorous comments short. You will lose listeners if they have to wait too long for punchlines.

-If you mess up somehow during your talk it's best to laugh at yourself a little and move on.

We will talk about that last point a little later on in this book. We will talk about not letting your mess-ups get the better of you.

Humor can make any dull topic a little more memorable. I am not implying that you might give dull presentations, but it's a good thing to keep in mind. If you loosen things up and basically give your audience permission to laugh and enjoy themselves, your presentation will be more memorable.

You can easily follow the suggestions in this section. I am sure you often speak to small groups maybe at work, or church, or at your book club. Try out these tips and see what happens. You will have positive results.

Stick around for the next session. We will discuss the importance of moving on after making mistakes and how to make sure a little flub doesn't throw you way off track.

It's quite simple. Say what you have to say and when you come to a sentence with a grammatical ending, sit down.
~ Winston Churchill

Make a mistake? Move on!

As a speaker, you will make mistakes. It WILL happen at some point and there's no way around it. When that happens – and the key word is WHEN – please know that you will survive and the world will continue to rotate on its axis. I could try and say something profound like "Well, just don't make mistakes. Be perfect!" But that's not possible. You WILL mess up and in this section you WILL learn how to move on from your flubs.

So what if you make a mistake? Remember that I mentioned earlier in the book that the audience won't hurt you. They're not going to pelt you with eggs if you mess up. But they will get annoyed if you make mistakes and keep calling attention to them. Remember to not do that.

Speech coach Nancy Tierney strongly believes – and I agree – that in the real world no one really cares if you flub or forget your words.

According to Tierney (2007): "The only time an audience is annoyed with such nonsense is if they feel that YOU are uncomfortable with what's happening. If you start feeling flustered and distracted by something unexpected, whether it's something you said or some other surprise, then your audience will feel that, too."

A few years ago, I was emceeing an awards program. My job was to introduce speakers and award winners and basically keep the program moving along. I had the list of names several days before the event and read everything over several times, including the morning of the event. Although, I do admit the last read-through was a fast one at the breakfast table.

When it came time to introduce one of the winners, I struggled with the gentleman's last name. I tried once. I tried twice. On the third try, I giggled slightly and said "That's what I get for not having enough coffee while reading through the script this morning!" People in the audience laughed and we moved on.

My point is that sometimes we can acknowledge our mistakes and make light of them. We don't have to dwell on them. Experts like Susan Tardanico, CEO and founding partner of the authentic leadership alliance, say if you mess up, make a tiny joke about it and move on. Don't fixate on mistakes.

"Your job is to close the gap, not widen it. By being self-effacing, humorous and real, you become approachable and it's easier to win over your audience. In turn, the more connected the audience feels to you, the more they'll pay attention to what you have to say," says Tardanico (2012).

What should you do if you mess up during your presentation? Here are some suggestions that will help you:

-Relax and forget about it. That's easier said than done but you can do it.

-Practice recovering from mistakes as quickly as you can.

-If you slur or speed over a name just repeat is slowly. Don't say "excuse me."

-Make a tiny joke about your blunder and keep going. Audience members are forgiving.

-If you made some type of mistake that hurt someone, privately apologize to them after the event.

-If you make an honest factual error in a presentation and someone calls you out on it, thank them and say that you will look into what they've told you.

-Try and be gracious when someone points out your mistakes. Don't be defensive even if they are being a jerk to you.

-The faster you bounce back from your error the faster the audience will forget.

-Keep your focus on the message to your audience and not on your mistakes.

-Own your flubs but know when to let go of them. Move ahead. You're human.

Without beating this message into the ground, I think what we've determined in this section is that everyone makes mistakes during speeches and presentations and can recover from them. You will make mistakes. You will recover from them too.

Did you ever play sports as a child, maybe baseball or softball? Did you ever have a ground ball roll right under your mitt and go through your legs? When that happens there's typically a coach nearby shouting "Don't worry! Get the next one!"

That's how you have to approach mistakes in speech making. Think of them as errors during a ballgame. If you make a mistake, get the next one and move along.

As we move along in this book, we are going to get physical. I don't mean there's strenuous physical exercise coming up. I mean that we are going to change our focus a little away from what you say and move over to how you say it and how you use your body during presentations.

It's not how strongly you feel about your topic, it's how strongly they feel about your topic after you speak.
~ Tim Salladay

WATCH YOUR BODY

Here's a little bit of history from back in the days when Richard Nixon and John Kennedy were running for the presidency.

Legend has it that on the way to their first televised debate, Nixon smacked his knee while getting out of his car. It hurt like crazy. Once he reached the studio, Nixon refused to wear makeup on TV. So, as the debate started Nixon was looking pale because he wasn't wearing makeup and he was noticeably leaning because of a sore knee. Nixon wore a painful look on his face the entire time. Kennedy was charming and smiling throughout.

After the debate, the pollsters went to work. Radio pollsters picked Nixon as the obvious winner. However, television pollsters said Kennedy won the debate. Many people believe Nixon's body language that he displayed on television helped contribute to Kennedy winning the election.

According to Emory University psychologist Steve Nowicki how people use their bodies during conversations and presentations plays a major role in whether speakers are connecting with their listeners: "Non-verbal communication is at least as important, if not more important, than the verbal part of relationships. When you break a non-verbal rule of language, it almost always has a negative emotional impact."

That makes sense.

Take into consideration what Steve Nowicki stated and use that in the Nixon/Kennedy example. You can see how his statement rings true. Non-verbal communication is EXTREMELY important when giving speeches or presentations. Notice how I capitalized EXTREMELY for EMPHASIS.

Someone can be giving the best presentation, as far as content goes, but if that person is avoiding eye contact, if he is slouching and not moving his hands or arms, if he is fussing with his shirt collar because it's too tight, all of those things will distract the listeners. Each physical faux pas will detract from the presentation and the presenter will not connect with the audience.

Don't be THAT guy. To avoid being that guy consider these non-verbal communication suggestions to help you connect with your audiences:

-Stand with confidence.

-Smile and use other positive facial expressions.

-Maintain eye contact with your audience.

-Maintain good posture. Don't slouch. Just like your mother told you.

-Avoid fidgeting with things like your necktie or jewelry. That will distract your listeners.

-Move around if you can.

-Remove barriers (like podiums) if possible to get you closer to your audience.

-Show your hands and keep them out of your pockets.

-Uncross your arms.

-Get physical. Use your hands, arms and facial expressions in your presentations.

-Use your voice correctly. Change your vocal tones when appropriate. Raise and lower your voice for emphasis at the right times.

Remember that following all of these suggestions will take time, practice and effort. If you are a normally shy person who struggles to make eye contact, then you will have to work very hard to break that bad habit. In time, you will.

If you are timid and want to stand behind the podium and use it as some sort of protection from the audience, put that podium aside if you can. Walk around and talk to your audience. It will make a stronger connection with your listeners.

If you have a habit of speaking in a monotone voice, you will have to break that bad habit too. Voice inflection has a great impact on our storytelling. By raising and lowering your voice at the right time, you will keep the interest of your listeners.

I hope that we all can agree that non-verbal communication plays a huge role in communication. We communicate with our voices and our bodies too. Use your bodies correctly and you will definitely have a more positive speaking experience. And your audiences will have a more positive listening experience. Trust me.

While we are on the subject, here's a non-verbal communication question: If you are giving a talk and the people in the audience are busy checking their watches or posting on Facebook, what is that telling you? Answer: It's telling you that you are probably talking too long.

In our next section, we are going to discuss the importance of watching the clock and respecting the listeners' time. They will be grateful when you do.

Please read on! I'll meet you at the next section...

No one ever complains about a speech being too short!
~ Ira Hayes

Watch the clock!

I don't want to waste time in this section and will get right to the point. Please respect the time of others when giving presentations. A long winded speaker is a really, really annoying speaker.

How many times have you watched the Academy Awards and seen an actor or actress get up on stage with a huge smile on their face and tears in their eyes and grab the Oscar after their name is announced. Then they begin to talk. And they talk. And they talk. The music starts to play and the actor/actress says "Oh gosh, I'm running out of time. I also want to thank the following 62 people…"

Actually, that's probably a bit harsh of me. In those situations, you can cut those people some slack. They've just one a major, career changing award and have not had time to collect their thoughts. So, if they ramble and seem unprepared, it is forgivable.

However, the same cannot be said for those folks who know they are going to speak, have been told how much time they have to fill, have time to prepare their speech, and THEN ramble on and on and go over their allotted time.

In the public speaking arena that is a sin.

Thou shalt not exceed your prearranged speaking time.

If you begin earning the reputation as a speaker who is long-winded and struggles to respect the clock, you might not be invited back and word could spread that you are a chatterbox who needs corralling. Don't let that happen.

Not long ago, I was emceeing an awards program where we were honoring some outstanding teachers. Prior to the event, we met with each teacher and explained that because there were so many teachers who were giving speeches that they had to limit their comments to two-minutes each in order to complete the program in a reasonable amount of time. Most of the teachers respected the time constraints. And you noticed I said most.

One teacher spoke for her assigned two-minutes and then pulled out a written speech that was almost three types pages long, single-spaced. She read the entire speech, which took her about eight-minutes. Her two-minute speech became a ten-minute speech. That was disrespectful to not only the organizers who asked her to be mindful of her time but also disrespectful to the people in the audience. Don't be that type of speaker.

Always, always, always respect the time of others when giving presentations.

Here are some things that you should keep in mind when giving a speech or presentation that will help you be more mindful of other people's time:

-Practice your presentation before your event and time yourself. (We've mentioned practice earlier in this book and will spend more time on that topic later.)

-If you notice during practice that your presentation is running long then find places where you can trim it.

-Come to your event prepared with your material.

-When you are at the podium, use a stopwatch and "watch the clock."

-If you are using PowerPoint, don't read every word on the slides. Hit some of the key points with each one of them. People can read your full presentation later if they want to do that.

-Stick to your message when you are speaking. Don't stray.

-Observe your audience as you watch the clock. If attendees start to fuss then you will know that you are probably speaking too long and losing their attention.

-If you feel you might be going too long, at some point you can ask someone "How much time do I have?"

-The event organizers will be more than happy to keep you on track.

-Respect people's time. They will appreciate it.

Here's one more suggestion that I would like you to consider: If you are asked to give a 20 minute presentation really make an effort to finish in less time, like fifteen to eighteen minutes. Going under your time budget creates an opportunity for questions from the audience at the end. Interaction with the audience will really add to your presentation.

So, please remember to outline your speech and pay attention to the length of it. Practice your speech. Time out how long it takes you to cover all of the information you are planning to share. Fine tune your presentation. When you give your speech, watch the clock. Also watch the audience. Know when to wrap things up and finish your talk.

This might seem a little overwhelming at first. It takes some time and practice to develop an internal clock. But if you do all of your preparation ahead of time and practice, chances are you will finish your presentation within the allotted time. Your event organizers will be grateful. Your audience will be especially grateful.

As you've noticed throughout this book, sometimes I mention "your notes" and sometimes I mention "your script." But which should you use? We will explore that topic in the next section.

I'll meet you on the next page.

It usually takes me more than three weeks to prepare a good impromptu speech.
~ Mark Twain

Use notes rather than scripts

It's been my experience that speeches are better when presenters speak from the heart, work from memory, or use notes or note cards. The second best speeches are those where presenters have a script with parts highlighted and use the script almost like notes. The worst speeches are those read word-for-word by the presenter.

Presenters who read straight from a piece of paper are boring speakers. People know you are reading to them and not really speaking to them. When I am in an audience listening to a presenter like this I often think "Just give me a copy of your script and I can read it later."

Basically, you have three options for presenting a speech:

-Read word-for-word from a script.

-Recite from memory.

-Use notes.

There are few presenters who can really get away with reading a speech verbatim: politicians, corporate leaders, and law enforcement personnel. Politicians reading a prepared text, either on print in front of them or on a teleprompter, have become accepted practice.

Corporate leaders can get away with sticking to their scripts when they have to read statements about things like product recalls that were written by their lawyers.

Law enforcement officials get a pass in this area too because when they hold news conferences, they have to read important facts and details. They have to get it right, so sticking to a script is okay in this situation.

However, passionate, off-the-cuff speakers are the best. There are several reasons why reading a script word for word is not a good idea in the majority of cases:

-It bores the audience. There are no dynamics.

-"Readers" often stumble over words or lose their place when they look up and back down at their script.

-People like presenters who <u>speak</u> to them and not <u>read</u> to them.

-Reading a speech is harder than just speaking unrehearsed.

-If you just read your speech, you can't gauge the reaction from audience members. That means you can't make adjustments.

Reciting from memory really isn't a good idea because the presenter comes off as stiff and unnatural. Remember when you were back in high school and you had to memorize and recite a poem in literature class? You stood up in front of the class and began spouting *The Road Not Taken* by Robert Frost. You were rolling right along until the third stanza when you said "And both that morning equally lay... um... And both that morning equally lay... I um... Aw, forget it..."

By then you wish you would have taken a road less travelled and sneaked out of the classroom.

The best speakers speak from the heart, sounding unrehearsed, or they work from notes or note cards. The good thing about working from notes is that your presentation comes off as more natural. When people are reading speeches, they are constantly filling the air with their words. Unless they lose their place and get flustered, there's never any silence and that's really not part of a normal conversation.

Jeff Haden, a contributor to Speakers, Inc. magazine, says presenters shouldn't feel the need to prattle endlessly. He says it's actually an effective technique to pause and wait. Haden (n.d.) says: "Pause for two or three seconds and the audience assumes you lost your place. Pause for five seconds and the audience begins to think the pause is intentional... and starts wondering why. Pause for ten seconds and even the people who were busy tweeting can't resist glancing up."

Practice a lot if you are going to use notes. Actually, practice a lot if you decide to go the full text script route. If you insist on working from a script, please look up at the audience frequently to make an effort to engage them. Look down and let your brain take in a few sentences and sections of text and repeat them as best as you can when you look back up. Either way, without practice you will find yourself fumbling through your presentation and you really want to avoid that.

The suggestions in this section are pretty clear. Using notes, using a full script, speaking spontaneously, or memorizing your material… it's all up to you and a personal decision only you can make.

If you are just starting out giving speeches, then maybe going the full script route is a good way to start. After you have some talks under your belt, you can start using notes or note cards. From there, you will evolve into a highly skilled speaker who can stand and deliver a wonderful presentation with nothing but a microphone to help you. Of course, that last scenario is a little down the road, but it is there waiting for you. Just give it time. It will happen.

Remember that you won't be able to deliver a wonderful presentation if your listeners aren't listening. If they don't feel a part of the presentation and they don't feel engaged, then you are really only speaking to yourself while a bunch of people watch. And you don't want that to happen.

In our next section, we discuss the importance of keeping your audience's attention.

The audience only pays attention as long
as you know where you are going.
~ Philip Crosby

Engage the audience

One of your primary objectives as a presenter is to get your audience locked in. You want to get and keep their attention. If you've sat through enough speeches and presentations, you know how easy it is to lose focus and let your mind wander.

You can prevent your listeners from contracting "Runaway Brain" if you work really hard to involve your audience cognitively and even physically. Some presenters like to throw in little exercises during their talks.

"Okay, will all the left-handed people stand up…"

"I want you to turn to the neighbor on your right, introduce yourself, and ask them…"

"We are going to do a writing exercise now, so please get out a piece of paper…"

I get to facilitate writing workshops and it's always a lot of fun. One exercise I often use near the beginning is to ask the participants to take out a sheet of paper and in five minutes write – and write legibly - a short story telling me about their name.

Where did their name come from? Is there a story behind their name? Do they like/hate their name? What does their name mean to them?

Then after five minutes, I ask the participants to exchange papers with someone sitting next to them and have that person read the story aloud. It's a great and fun ice breaker and it really begins to engage the participants. Sometimes that can be challenging.

Presentations are much more interesting for people on the receiving end if people on the presenting end engage the audience in some way, whether through questions and answers or full-scale participation, like being asked to stand up and interact with each other, or move around.

Forbes writer Kristi Hedges agrees with that approach. She once wrote: "People will pay attention if they know that at some point, they'll have to participate. And providing the audience the opportunity to interact with each other adds a peer learning dimension to a presentation (2014)." And I can't agree with her more on that point.

Here are some tips for keeping your audience engaged. They should look familiar because we have been exploring all of these ideas throughout this book:

-Know your audience and make sure the information you deliver is appropriate for the group and on-point.

-Know your material. Make sure you are well-versed in the content you are sharing. However, remember that you are probably not the smartest person in the room and someone will know if you are faking.

-Know the room and use the size and arrangement of it to your advantage.

-Tell them what you are going to tell them. Tell them. Then tell them what you told them. People like this kind of organized presentation.

-Keep it simple and don't try to impress people with how smart you are because that will only turn off your listeners.

-Imagine yourself giving a really, really good speech. Then give a really good speech. Visualization helps.

-Be happy to be there because your listeners will know right away if you are not.

-Calm down. No one's going to hurt you. Once you realize that you will be able to relax and settle down.

-The people listening want to like you. That means all you have to do to win them over is to reinforce their reasons for liking you by doing a good and thorough job.

-Use personal stories because the audience members want to know more about you and how your personal experiences inspired the event organizers to ask you to be their speaker.

-Use humor because people want to enjoy themselves and laugh. If you make people laugh, they will remember that good feeling and associate that good feeling with you.

-Make a mistake? Move on! Why? Everyone makes mistakes and if you dwell on yours while you are standing behind the podium it will have a negative impact on your performance.

-Watch your body language. Speakers transmit equally effective messages with their bodies. Using the proper body language keeps listeners engaged and interested in what you have to say.

-Watch the clock because there are few things worse than listening to a speaker go on and on, well past the allotted time. Remember time is valuable and you have to respect the time of the people in your audience. They will appreciate you for it.

-Use notes rather than scripts because it will help your speech come off as more natural and less rehearsed. That will make your audience feel more at ease and more ready to soak in all of the great information you are sharing with them.

Here's another suggestion to consider: With the infusion of social media, many presenters are also engaging audiences through social media DURING their talks. That's something you can consider. If you want to build interaction, you can do it in person or via the Internet. You can suggest that people tweet their questions to you if they are reluctant to ask publicly.

The only downfall to that suggestion is that you risk losing listeners to their cellphones and wireless tablets. They might drift out onto the Internet and never come back. But some presenters think it's worth the risk.

As you might have guessed, engaging an audience can be challenging. Like everything else with public speaking, it takes some effort. However, if you follow the suggestions in the list above, you have a really good chance at keeping your audiences focused on you. You are probably willing to take those steps because you've purchased this book and have read this far. You are invested in this. Good for you.

That personal investment continues in the next section where we will discuss the importance of practice and more practice. Read on!

Extemporaneous speaking should be practiced and cultivated.
~ Abraham Lincoln

Practice. A lot. And then practice some more.

By now, you might have heard of what's referred as the 10,000 hours rule. That's the rule that states if you practice something, anything for 10,000 hours that you will become an expert at it. Not everyone buys into this theory but it makes sense. The biggest caveat to it is this: Who has 10,000 hours to dedicate to anything?

In regard to the topic of this book, who might have 10,000 hours of public speaking experience?

While setting aside 10,000 hours for public speaking rehearsal is unrealistic, we all can agree that practice makes perfect. Or at least practice makes for "very good" at the very least.

If you are scheduled to give a speech, or some sort of presentation, do a 3-to-1 practice schedule. That means you should run through your speech at least three times for every time you are going to present it. It might not be 10,000 hours' worth but it's a practice that has worked for me over the years.

Experienced speakers sing the praises of practice. David Brooks, from Toastmasters International, strongly believes that rehearsal and practice lead to a well-received presentation.

"Few people speak well extemporaneously," says Brooks (n.d.). "The greatest speakers you have ever heard are the ones who have expended the greatest effort. Speaking is a skill that takes practice."

So, how and where can you get the chance to practice your public speaking so that you can sharpen your skills? That's a logical question. Here is a list of helpful suggestions:

-Ask if you can give a presentation at work. Start small and move up from there.

-If you are a PTA member, or belong to some other type of group, volunteer to lead a meeting discussion or ask to make a presentation. It's a good start.

-Attend public meetings. Raise your hand to ask a question or offer a comment. It's not the same as making a speech but it is speaking in public. Think baby steps.

-Join a local group like the Rotary Club or Toastmasters where members join for the purpose of polishing their presentation skills. There are a lot of nice people in these groups and they are extremely supportive of each other.

-Read your speech or notes over and over until you are confident in knowing the material.

-Find a quiet and private place to practice your presentation aloud.

-Use a stopwatch to time yourself to make sure you are within your assigned time limit.

-Stand up when you practice.

-Practice your facial and hand gestures so that you get comfortable using them during your talk.

-Record your speech with a video camera or audio recorder, play it back, and then do it again. Lather. Rinse. Repeat.

-Practice your speech in front of a friend or family member. Insist on honest feedback.

-Use that feedback to improve your presentation.

Some people often suggest that you practice on front of a mirror. That might work for some folks but I've always found that method to be a little distracting. If I am practicing alone, I would rather speak aloud and look at a wall rather than myself in the mirror. But if you give that idea a try and it works for you, that's great.

There's one other place where you can practice public speaking and that is in the privacy of your own car. I've done this myself. While driving to an event, if I have some prepared remarks that I want to go over, I plug in my hands-free gadget into my phone and talk while in the car.

Look around when you are stopped at a red light. People are talking on their phones, hopefully using a hands-free device. People in the other cars likely won't give you any strange looks – if they look your way at all – because they are probably talking to someone on the phones too. Give it a try and see if you feel comfortable doing this. I find that it works.

So, in this section we've learned that there are a lot of ways that you can get public speaking practice. Try a handful of the suggestions from the list above.

Remember that practice is what you need to become a polished presenter. I know this interests you enough that you will follow up on some of these suggestions. If you do follow through you will be well on your way to becoming the public speaker that you want to be. It takes time. It takes effort. And I am confident you are willing and eager to make that kind of personal investment.

Our next, and final section, is where we stick the landing, to use a gymnastics phrase. It's my final pep talk to you to get you out there and talking.

As long as there are human rights to be defended; as long as there are great interests to be guarded; as long as the welfare of nations is a matter for discussion, so long will public speaking have its place.
~ William Jennings Bryan

Speak in public as much as you can

This is my final push –at least consider it my friendly final nudge – to get you out there and presenting.

Please don't ever let anyone tell you that public speaking isn't important because it is. In fact, getting up in front of a group of people of any size is one of the most important skills a person can own.

I wasn't a good public speaker at first. No one is. Remember that story I shared at the very beginning of this book about how I learned to be a lector in church and read the scripture in front of a congregation when I was in the third grade? Do you think I was good at it right away? I wasn't.

Do you think the first time I was the emcee at an awards banquet that everything went off without a hitch? I was really nervous but learned to plow through.

The more public speaking opportunities I took advantage of the better I became. The same will happen for you.

You can use solid public speaking skills in both your personal and professional lives. Public speaking will help you sharpen your everyday verbal and non-verbal communication skills. That will help you become successful on both a personal and professional level.

And you want to be successful.

We've already established that speaking in front of a group of people is one of the world's most common fears. You might even feel this way and that's why you've been reading this book. Please know that becoming an effective presenter will increase your self-confidence. If you master this challenging skill, imagine what other personal hurdles you will be able to clear.

You want more self-confidence.

Becoming a stronger public speaker will make you more comfortable around other people, especially strangers. Once you grow as a presenter, it'll be nothing for you to meet new people and speak with them.

You want to feel comfortable meeting new people.

Public speaking ability is a real career booster.

You want to advance in your career.

Remember that at some point in your life you will have to get involved in some type of public speaking. Your boss will want you to give a presentation on that new project. Your pastor will ask you to lead a discussion on a new church program. Your teacher will require you to explain your paper's thesis to the rest of the class. The list of reasons and opportunities is endless.

I strongly suggest that you join groups and organizations that encourage members to develop and fine-tune public speaking skills. For example, Toastmasters International is a great organization that promotes public speaking. The same goes for your local Rotary Club. These groups are steeped in public speaking tradition.

You also can go online and look for any local Meetup groups in your area that specifically focus on public speaking. You'll have a lot in common with other people in the group. You will meet new friends AND develop your communication skills. That is quite a combination!

So, go out and speak. Speak to small groups. Speak to large groups. Start presenting. Begin small and build from there. Take what you've learned, apply it, and keep applying it.

Good luck! You'll do well.

Speak clearly, if you speak at all; carve every word before you let it fall.
~ Oliver Wendell Holmes

About the author

Here's a little bit of information about me. I am a Communications Director, author, free-lance writer college writing and communications instructor, and a former journalist and radio talk show host.

I worked for 22 years in the journalism business, with most of that time spent honing my public speaking skills in television and radio.

For more than 12 years, I was a reporter and anchor at KCRA-TV in Sacramento where I was fortunate to have earned 14 prestigious journalism awards. I have also worked as a television and radio reporter and anchor in Dallas-Fort Worth and Pittsburgh.

In 2003, I was a runner-up for the Will Rogers Humanitarian Award, presented by the National Society of Newspaper Columnists. I have a B.A. in Journalism from Penn State University and an M.A. in Strategic Communications from National University.

I also have extensive experience in media relations having served as Communications Director for several agencies for the State of California, including the Department of Consumer Affairs and the Department of Conservation.

I currently serve as the Communications Director for the Sacramento County Office of Education where I have been fortunate to have earned numerous awards from the California School Public Relations Association (CalSPRA).

For more information visit my Web site: www.timherrera.com.

Tim's other books

Media Relations: A Guide to Giving Great Interviews

What the Online Student MUST Know: Vital Lessons BEFORE Logging On

30 Things You Should Know About Media Relations, 2nd Edition

30 Things You Should Know About Media Relations, 1st Edition

Dad, You Are NOT Going Out Wearing That!

From Wedgies to Feeding Frenzies

Where the Dust Never Settles

I'm Their Dad! Not Their Babysitter!

Thank you!

I want to thank you for taking the time to read this book. It means a lot to me. I believe this book will help you strengthen your public speaking skills.

I plan on updating this book from time to time. If you have some suggestions for me and would like to suggest a topic, please feel free to send me an email at timherrera@rocketmail.com.

I also would appreciate it if you had the time to write a review of this book on Amazon. The will also let me know what additional information readers would like to see in this good.

Best of luck to you!

Tim

References

Altucher, J. (n.d.). How To Be The Best Public Speaker on the Planet. . Retrieved July 1, 2014, from http://www.jamesaltucher.com/2013/10/how-to-be-the-best-public-speaker-on-the-planet/

Baldoni, J. (2012, May 4). Give a Great Speech: 3 Tips from Aristotle Read more: http://www.inc.com/john-baldoni/deliver-a-great-speech-aristotle-three-tips.html#ixzz36FJv8Kec. *Inc.*.

Brooks, D. (n.d.). For the Novice: Seven Staples of Public Speaking. . Retrieved July 1, 2014, from http://www.toastmasters.org/ToastmastersMagazine/ToastmasterArchive/2008/August/Departments/FortheNovice.aspx

Clark, C. (2011, March 22). Top 10 facts about non-verbal communication. . Retrieved July 5, 2014, from http://esciencecommons.blogspot.com/2011/03/key-facts-about-nonverbal-communication.html

Clendenin, R. (n.d.). 21 Tips For Overcoming Fear of Public Speaking . . Retrieved July 2, 2014, from http://happysimplelife.com/21-tips-for-overcoming-fear-of-public-speaking/

Cooke, J. (n.d.). How to Add Humor to Any Speech. . Retrieved July 1, 2014, from http://www.toastmasters.org/ToastmastersMagazine/ToastmasterArchive/2007/March/AddHumor.aspx

DeNoon, D. (2006, April 20). Fear of Public Speaking Hardwired. . Retrieved July 1, 2014, from http://www.webmd.com/anxiety-panic/guide/20060420/fear-public-speaking

Haden, J. (n.d.). 5 Ways to Become a Better Speaker Overnight. . Retrieved July 1, 2014, from https://www.linkedin.com/today/post/article/20130612120408-20017018-5-ways-to-become-a-better-speaker-overnight

Hall-Flavin, D. (2014, February 25). How can I overcome my fear of public speaking?. . Retrieved July 1, 2014, from http://www.mayoclinic.org/diseases-conditions/phobias/expert-answers/fear-of-public-speaking/faq-20058416

Hedges, K. (2014, January 28). Five Easy Tricks To Make Your Presentation Interactive. . Retrieved July 2, 2014, from http://www.forbes.com/sites/work-in-progress/2014/01/28/five-easy-tricks-to-make-your-presentation-interactive/

Mitchell, O. (2009, September 22). The three causes of public speaking fear (and what you can do about them). . Retrieved July 1, 2014, from http://www.speakingaboutpresenting.com/nervousness/fear-of-public-speaking-causes/

Mitchell, O. (2009, October 2). The truth about visualization for public speaking success. . Retrieved July 1, 2014, from http://www.speakingaboutpresenting.com/nervousness/visualization-public-speaking/

Ricci, T. (2012, August 1). Public Speaking: Know Your Audience. . Retrieved July 1, 2014, from https://www.asme.org/career-education/articles/public-speaking/public-speaking-know-your-audience

Smith, J. (2013, August 13). How To Give A Great Speech. . Retrieved July 2, 2014, from http://www.forbes.com/sites/jacquelynsmith/2013/08/13/how-to-give-a-great-speech-3/

Tardanico, S. (2012, May 29). Want To Be A Better Public Speaker? Do What The Pros Do... Retrieved July 1, 2014, from http://www.forbes.com/sites/susantardanico/2012/05/29/want-to-be-a-better-public-speaker-do-what-the-pros-do/

Tierney, N. (2007, August 14). Public Speaking and The Myth of Making Mistakes. . Retrieved , from http://ezinearticles.com/?Public-Speaking-and-The-Myth-of-Making-Mistakes&id=688187

Witt, C. (2013, April 16). The First Rule for Telling Personal Stories in a Speech. . Retrieved July 1, 2014, from http://christopherwitt.com/the-first-rule-for-telling-personal-stories-in-a-speech/

Witt, C. (n.d.). How to Plan a Speech. . Retrieved July 1, 2014, from http://www.wittcom.com/how_to_plan_a_speech.htm

Zeoli, R. (2014, April 16). Seven Principles of Effective Public Speaking. . Retrieved July 1, 2014, from http://www.amanet.org/training/articles/Seven-Principles-of-Effective-Public-Speaking.aspx

www.ingramcontent.com/pod-product-compliance
Lightning Source LLC
Chambersburg PA
CBHW051524170526
45165CB00002B/595